MW01278414

SPOTLIGHT ON NATURE
ELEPHANT

MELISSA GISH

CREATIVE EDUCATION · CREATIVE PAPERBACKS

Published by Creative Education and Creative Paperbacks
P.O. Box 227, Mankato, Minnesota 56002
Creative Education and Creative Paperbacks are imprints
of The Creative Company
www.thecreativecompany.us

Design and production
by Chelsey Luther
Art direction by Rita Marshall
Printed in the United States of America

Photographs by Alamy (M & J Bloomfield, Choups, John Crux, Martin Har-
vey, imageBROKER, Images of Africa Photobank, Ernie James, mauritius
images GmbH, Johan Swanepoel), Dreamstime (Clickit, Feathercollector,
Simon Fletcher, Isselee, Jakub Krechowicz, Vinesh Kumar), Getty Images
(Digital Zoo/DigitalVision, Anup Shah/DigitalVision, David Suttinger/
EyeEm), iStockphoto (ivstiv), Minden Pictures (Jean-Jacques Alcalay,
Richard Du Toit, Anup Shah/NPL), National Geographic Creative (Frans
Lanting), Shutterstock (Dashu, Daxio Productions, THPStock)

Copyright © 2020 Creative Education, Creative Paperbacks
International copyright reserved in all countries. No part of this book may be
reproduced in any form without written permission from the publisher.

Library of Congress Cataloging-in-Publication Data
Names: Gish, Melissa, author.
Title: Elephant / Melissa Gish.
Series: Spotlight on nature.
Includes index.
Summary: A detailed chronology of developmental milestones drives this life
study of elephants, including their habitats, physical features, and conserva-
tion measures taken to protect these lumbering land animals.
Identifiers: LCCN 2018041002 / ISBN 978-1-64026-182-2 (hardcover) /
ISBN 978-1-62832-745-8 (pbk) / ISBN 978-1-64000-300-2 (eBook)
Subjects: LCSH: African elephant—Zimbabwe—Juvenile literature. / Hwange
National Park (Zimbabwe)—Juvenile literature / Elephants—Zimbabwe.
Classification: LCC QL737.P98 G57 2019 / DDC 599.67/409689—dc23

First Edition HC 9 8 7 6 5 4 3 2 1
First Edition PBK 9 8 7 6 5 4 3 2 1

CONTENTS

AFRICAN BUSH ELEPHANTS

of Hwange National Park

In western Zimbabwe, Hwange (*WAHN-gay*) National Park covers 5,657 square miles (14,652 sq km) of grasslands and seasonal wetlands. The park is home to more than 500 different kinds of birds and **mammals**. During the day, African wild dogs patrol the landscape, while lions doze in the shade of giraffe thorn trees. Later, as darkness falls, spotted hyenas and leopards begin the hunt for small antelope. Moonlight glistens off the surface of a small pond. Nearby, a herd of elephants has gathered.

It is mid-October, the dry season. The elephants press close, swaying and bumping one another. They snort and rumble nervously. Something is about to happen, and they don't want to miss it. At the center of the herd is a pregnant female whose body is swollen with the baby she has been carrying for nearly two years. The time for her calf to be born has finally arrived.

CLOSE-UP

Quiet feet

Elephants walk silently because the soles of their feet are filled with shock-absorbing fatty tissue. This tissue smothers the sounds of breaking twigs and dry grass underfoot.

CHAPTER ONE
LIFE BEGINS

Elephants are the world's largest land animals. Two of the three species live in Africa. Most African bush elephants roam the grasslands of Botswana, Kenya, Namibia, South Africa, Tanzania, and Zimbabwe. African forest elephants live primarily in the forests of Gabon, southern Cameroon, and northern Democratic Republic of Congo. The Asian elephant is divided into three subspecies based on geographic location. The Sri Lankan elephant and the Sumatran elephant are named for their island homes. The Indian elephant is found in 11 countries throughout Southeast Asia. Scientists are debating whether a small number of elephants living on the island of Borneo should be considered a fourth subspecies.

HWANGE NATIONAL PARK AFRICAN BUSH ELEPHANT MILESTONES

DAY (1)

- Born
- Coarse, wiry hair on head and back
- Begins walking
- Weight: 200 pounds (90.7 kg)
- Height: 3 feet (0.9 m) at the shoulder

FEATURED FAMILY

Welcome to the World

In Hwange National Park, the 30-year-old female elephant is breathing heavily. A dozen other elephants surround her, including her two older offspring. She groans and bends her back legs. Her herd mates squeal and rumble with excitement. Moments later, the baby elephant slips from its mother's body and tumbles to the soft, dry earth. It has been a long pregnancy. Elephants carry their babies for 22 months—longer than any other animal. The newborn female calf wriggles in the grass, stretching her legs for the first time.

Elephant mothers normally give birth to one baby, called a calf. Twins occur rarely. Calves can usually rise to their feet and walk within an hour of birth. Newborns stand about 3 feet (0.9 m) tall and weigh between 170 and 265 pounds (77.1–120 kg), with males being heavier than females. Mother elephants feed their calves milk. Calves typically nurse for 4 years or as many as 10, if their mother does not have another calf. Short calves may need to balance on their hind legs to reach their mother's milk. Calves begin to eat grass and leaves when they are a few months old. All elephants are herbivores. This means they eat only plants, leaves, grasses, seeds, and fruits.

CLOSE-UP
Flexible trunk

An elephant's trunk has more than 40,000 muscles and tendons. Elephants breathe through two nostrils in the trunk. The trunk's tip has fingerlike parts that can grasp and pick up things.

(3) **MONTHS**

First taste of grass and leaves
Weight: 380 pounds (172 kg)

Because of their size, adult elephants have no natural enemies. However, calves are vulnerable, especially as newborns. Crocodiles, lions, and hyenas in Africa and tigers in Asia are the main threats. Elephants live in family groups called herds. The entire herd never sleeps at the same time. While some elephants sleep for one to three hours, a few stand guard against predators. Calves sleep up to five hours. To protect the herd's calves, elephants may charge at enemies, kicking them or bashing them with their heavy trunks.

CLOSE-UP
Replaceable teeth

Elephants normally have 26 teeth, including 2 tusks. All but the tusks are replaced up to five times in an elephant's lifetime. Tusks are filled with nerves, so breaking a tusk is painful.

——— FEATURED FAMILY ———

First Meal

The calf was born with four teeth. In two to three months, they will be used to grind up grass and leaves. For now, though, she consumes only her mother's milk, drinking more than 10 quarts (9.5 l) a day. She gains about 15 pounds (6.8 kg) per week on the nutrient-rich milk. When the calf is about six months old, more teeth will grow, including two stubby tusks called tushes. These will be replaced by permanent tusks. Tusks will grow two to seven inches (5.1–17.8 cm) per year until they are about six feet (1.8 m) long.

Because of their size, adult elephants have

NO
NATURAL ENEMIES.

(6) **MONTHS**

> Tusks are first visible
> Weight: 470 pounds (213 kg)

CLOSE-UP
Skin protection

Elephants seek out water not only for drinking but also for bathing. A coating of mud protects their skin from sunburn, and an extra layer of dry dirt provides relief from biting insects.

CHAPTER TWO

EARLY ADVENTURES

Mother elephants teach their offspring how to survive. A calf learns to use its trunk to pick up things, scratch its ears, and suck up water for a drink. By mimicking its mother, a calf learns how to take a dust bath and flap its ears to cool down. It learns to recognize communication that signals safety, excitement, and danger. Mothers also teach calves how to select the best food. An adult elephant may eat up to 500 pounds (227 kg) of food and drink about 50 gallons (189 l) of water each day. To reach a water source, elephants may have to walk great distances. For this reason, elephants typically give birth just before the rainy season. This gives calves time to grow strong enough to keep up with the herd when it next travels to find food and water.

9 MONTHS

- Learns to use trunk to dust bathe
- Plays with other calves but stays close to mother

1 YEAR

- Has full control of trunk
- As a female, weighs half as much as males her age
- Weight: 690 pounds (313 kg)
- Height: 4 feet (1.2 m) at the shoulder

CLOSE-UP
Strong sniffers
Elephants have a powerful sense of smell. They sniff through their nostrils. Millions of scent-detecting cells help identify the source. They can smell water up to 12 miles (19.3 km) away.

— FEATURED FAMILY —

Look Who's Traveling

During Hwange's dry season, temperatures soar above 105 °F (40.6 °C). The grass is brown, and the pools are dry. The elephants must travel across the parched landscape to find food and water. The calf, now almost a year old, works hard to keep up with her mother. Her two older brothers walk ahead with the rest of the herd. Suddenly, a pair of spotted hyenas appears. They spot the calf and begin yipping, calling for backup. The elephants trumpet angrily and rush to surround the calf. Her mother charges toward the hyenas. The predators jump back, yipping wildly. This calf is too well-protected. The hyenas abandon their plan for attack and disappear into the tall grass.

Elephants can smell water up to
TWELVE
MILES AWAY.

(3) **YEARS**

▸ Feeds mostly on vegetation
▸ Nurses less frequently
▸ Body hair more sparse
▸ Weight: 1,670 pounds (757 kg)

Elephants walk about four miles (6.4 km) per hour. An elephant herd may travel around a territory greater than 1,200 square miles (3,108 sq km), following the same routes year after year.

Female elephants run herds that usually consist of 4 to 12 related females, young males, and calves. These matriarchal herds may grow to include up to 70 elephants from different families. Male elephants either live in groups called bull bands or live alone. If a herd gets too big and resources become scarce, some members may break away to form a new herd. The new herd then moves to a different territory.

CLOSE-UP
Keeping cool

Elephant skin is more than one inch (2.5 cm) thick, except on and behind the ears. There it is as thin as paper. Elephants cool their bodies by flapping their ears. This cools the blood under the thin skin.

FEATURED FAMILY

Give It a Try

At 16 months old, the elephant calf is enjoying her second rainy season. The savanna is a rich, green pasture. The elephants forage almost constantly—about 80 percent of their day. The calf's mouth is full of chewing teeth. Her permanent tusks have begun to grow on either side of her trunk. She watches her mother reach among the sharp spines of a grapple plant and pluck a long, curved fruit. Then the calf eagerly jumps forward to give it a try.

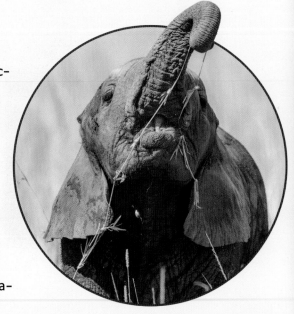

⑤ YEARS

- ▸ Starts to forage farther from mother
- ▸ Tusks are 18 inches (45.7 cm) long
- ▸ Weight: 2,650 pounds (1,202 kg)
- ▸ Height: 5 feet (1.5 m) at the shoulder

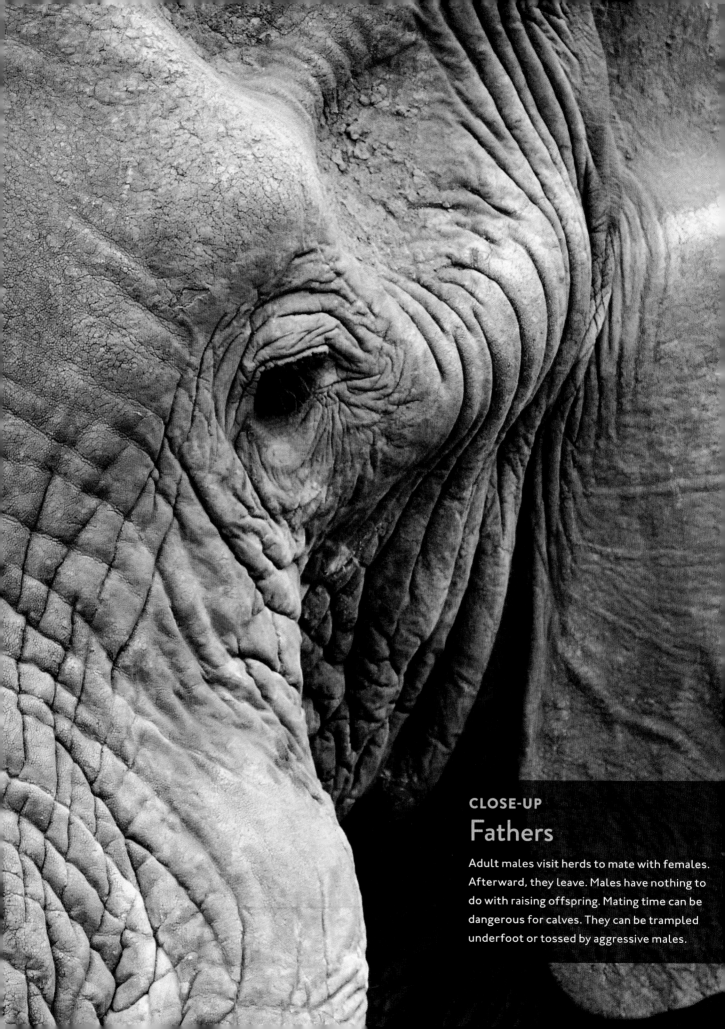

CLOSE-UP
Fathers

Adult males visit herds to mate with females. Afterward, they leave. Males have nothing to do with raising offspring. Mating time can be dangerous for calves. They can be trampled underfoot or tossed by aggressive males.

CHAPTER THREE

LIFE LESSONS

The three elephant species have adapted to life in different habitats. African bush elephants have thicker, more wrinkly skin than their cousins. This is because they spend much of their time on the open plains under the hot sun. The wrinkles trap moisture and distribute heat more efficiently to help the elephants stay cool. Bush elephants also have the largest tusks. A pair of male bush elephants' tusks may be as heavy as 220 pounds (99.8 kg) and nearly 8 feet (2.4 m) long. Elephants use their tusks to tear up roots, dig for water, and defend themselves. African forest elephants have shorter, thinner, and straighter tusks, which makes maneuvering through trees and underbrush less cumbersome. Forest elephants are about three feet (0.9 m) shorter than their cousins on the savanna.

6 YEARS

- Fully weaned
- Helps protect younger sibling
- Weight: 3,200 pounds (1,451 kg)

17 YEARS

- Reaches maturity
- Tusks are five feet (1.5 m) long
- Stays with mother; males her age leave the herd

CLOSE-UP
Communication waves

Elephants squeal, rumble, and trumpet. They also use infrasound. These sound waves are so low that humans can't hear them. Scientists believe these sounds can travel as far as six miles (9.7 km).

FEATURED FAMILY

This Is How It's Done

In Hwange National Park, the calf is nearing her third birthday. Her mother is using her tusks to peel bark from an acacia tree—a healthy snack. The calf munches fallen bark. Suddenly, a thunderous trumpet echoes across the savanna: a male elephant is approaching the herd. The calf's mother will soon be ready to mate again. Ignoring the sound, the calf sets to work using one of her own tusks to scrape the tree. Her tusks are only three inches (7.6 cm) long, but she persists.

AFRICAN ELEPHANT   ASIAN ELEPHANT

The easiest way to tell African from Asian elephants is by looking at the ears. African elephants have large ears that extend above the neck. Asian elephants have much smaller ears. Also, Asian elephants are sheltered from the sun in their forest environment, so their skin is less wrinkly. And unlike African elephants, Asian elephants may change color. As they age, their skin may fade from gray to pink, especially on the ears and trunk.

Elephants are some of Earth's most intelligent and emotional animals. Studies have shown they can recognize themselves in a mirror. This demonstrates that they have a sense of their own identity—something rare in the animal world. And elephants express emotions

 YEARS

- Full-grown; males continue to gain weight over lifetime
- Mates for the first time

- Weight: 6,400 pounds (2,903 kg)
- Height: 6 feet (1.8 m) at the shoulder

such as joy, sadness, sympathy, and empathy. Research on a herd of elephants in Thailand showed that whenever an elephant was distressed, its herd mates would quietly rumble and chirp while rubbing their trunks on the distressed elephant's face and mouth—as if reassuring their sad friend. Elephants also express altruism. Numerous studies have documented stronger elephants helping weaker or injured elephants. Such behavior is also rare in the animal kingdom, yet it is fundamental to life in an elephant herd.

CLOSE-UP
Ears of all shapes

African elephants' ears can be six feet (1.8 m) tall. Bush elephants have triangular-shaped ears with pointy ends, while forest elephants have more rounded ears. Asian elephants' ears are only two feet (0.6 m) long.

──── **FEATURED FAMILY** ────

Practice Makes Perfect

The herd gathers around a community watering hole. Zebras, wildebeest, bushbuck, and other gregarious animals share space at the water's edge. When the elephants have drunk their fill, the calf follows her mother into the pool. They stir up the mud with their feet. The calf mimics her mother, sucking up muddy water in her trunk and then spraying it over her back. She squeals and dashes back to the shallow edge of the pool. She flops down and rolls on her back, covering herself in thick, protective mud.

STRONGER
elephants help WEAKER or INJURED elephants.

48 YEARS

70 YEARS

Gives birth to last calf

End of life

CHAPTER FOUR

ELEPHANT SPOTTING

Elephants worldwide are in serious trouble. As humans expand farms and cities, elephants' natural habitat is destroyed. Meanwhile, climate change contributes to extended periods of drought and shifting growing seasons, affecting elephants' food and water resources. But the greatest threat by far is the illegal hunting, or poaching, of elephants for their tusks, hide, and meat. At least 30,000 elephants are illegally killed each year. All elephants are in danger of becoming extinct. Once numbering in the millions, only about 300,000 African bush elephants and about 100,000 African forest elephants exist today. Fewer than 45,000 Asian elephants remain.

Trained, performing elephants were once a cornerstone of circuses and traveling exhibits. Today, however, elephants are being removed from the spotlight as people have come to learn that the best place to appreciate elephants is in the wild. North American zoos exhibit fewer than 300 elephants. New insights into the needs of elephants—including vast areas to roam and large social groups—have led many zoos to turn their elephants over to more spacious zoos and sanctuaries. The Elephant Sanctuary in Hohenwald, Tennessee, is one such place. It provides elephants with 2,700 acres (1,093 ha) of grassland and forest, heated barns, and privacy. The sanctuary is closed to the public. People can only watch the elephants via live streaming video.

The National Zoo in Washington, D.C., and the San Diego Zoo Safari Park house elephants that visitors can watch via the Elephant Cam on the zoos' websites. Both zoos participate in conservation programs that provide funding as well as scientists to conduct research on elephants in their native lands. Twenty-one national parks and wildlife sanctuaries cover more than 5.6 million acres (2.3 million ha) of Asia's Dawna Tenasserim Landscape. These parks and sanctuaries provide legally protected forest habitat for hundreds of Indian elephants and other animals in Thailand and Myanmar.

Since 1975, Dr. Joyce Poole has studied African elephants. Today, Poole continues to collaborate with the Amboseli Elephant Research Project in Kenya's Amboseli National Park. Their research has led to invaluable discoveries about the relationships and social behaviors of elephants, as well as their reproductive patterns and communication. Understanding how elephants live can allow scientists and conservationists to determine what elephants need to survive. As we learn more about elephants, we can take further steps toward finding ways to protect them and preserve their way of life for the future.

SNAPSHOTS

Male **African bush elephants** are the largest of all elephants. They can be nearly 13 feet (4 m) tall at the shoulder and can weigh up to 16,000 pounds (7,257 kg).

African forest elephants typically stand about 8 feet (2.4 m) tall at the shoulder and weigh about 8,500 pounds (3,856 kg).

The largest known **Asian elephant** to have ever lived was Raja Gaj, who stood 11.2 feet (3.4 m) tall. He lived in Nepal's Bardiya National Park. When last seen in 2007, he was believed to be 70 years old.

Fewer than 3,000 **Sumatran elephants** still exist. Researchers fear that habitat destruction and poaching will soon drive these elephants to extinction.

African forest elephants travel in groups of two to eight relatives—much smaller than the herds of their cousins living on the savannas.

Only about 1,600 **Borneo pygmy elephants** exist. They are about 20 percent smaller than elephants on the Asian mainland. They have long tails that may reach to the ground.

Forest elephants have five toenails on the front foot and four on the back foot, whereas **bush elephants** have four toenails on the front foot and three on the back foot.

The tips of **African elephants'** trunks have two flap-like parts that are used like fingers, while **Asian elephants'** trunks have one.

Pygmy elephants are African forest elephants that grow smaller than normal because of genetic mutations. They weigh less than 2,000 pounds (907 kg).

In 1882, P. T. Barnum's Greatest Show on Earth debuted an **African bush elephant**. His stage name, Jumbo, became a common synonym for "very big."

Sri Lankan elephants are the largest subspecies of Asian elephant. They can grow to 11 feet (3.4 m) tall at the shoulder and weigh 6 tons (5.4 t).

ECHO

Animal behaviorist Cynthia Moss spent 30 years studying Echo, an **African bush elephant** matriarch who was featured in several books and documentaries. Echo died in 2009 at the age of 65.

Ruby was an **Asian elephant** who lived at the Phoenix Zoo from 1974 until her death in 1998. She was well known for painting pictures, holding the brush in her trunk.

WORDS to Know

altruism   the act of helping another without expecting anything in return

extinct   died off completely; having no living members

genetic mutations   distinct forms resulting from changes to genes (the basic physical units of heredity)

gregarious   instinctively seeking the cooperation and company of others in a large group

mammals   animals that have a backbone and hair or fur, give birth to fully formed offspring, and produce milk to feed their young

nerves   fibers that carry sensations to the brain and impulses from the brain to other body parts

nutrient   a substance that gives a living thing energy and helps it grow

savanna   a grassy, mostly treeless plain in tropical or subtropical regions

species   a group of living beings with shared characteristics and the ability to reproduce with one another

territory   an area owned or claimed and defended from intruders

LEARN MORE

Books

Bell, Samantha S. *The Amazing Social Lives of African Elephants*. Mankato, Minn.: Child's World, 2018.

Blewett, Ashlee Brown, and Daniel Raven-Ellison. *Mission: Elephant Rescue: All about Elephants and How to Save Them*. Washington, D.C.: National Geographic, 2014.

Prokos, Anna. *Elephants*. New York: Children's Press, 2018.

Websites

"Asian Elephant." National Geographic Kids. https://kids.nationalgeographic.com/animals/mammals/asian-elephant/.

"Elephant." San Diego Zoo Animals & Plants. https://animals.sandiegozoo.org/animals/elephant.

"Elephant." WWF. https://www.worldwildlife.org/species/elephant.

Documentaries

Bowie, Ben, and Geoff Luck. *Naledi: A Baby Elephant's Tale*. Vulcan Productions, 2016.

Schatz, Amy. *An Apology to Elephants*. Home Box Office (HBO), 2013.

Stevens, Jan. *Walking with Elephants*. Boiler Media, 2014.

Note: Every effort has been made to ensure that any websites listed above were active at the time of publication. However, because of the nature of the Internet, it is impossible to guarantee that these sites will remain active indefinitely or that their contents will not be altered.

Visit

AFRICAN LION SAFARI

This drive-through park is home to more than 1,000 exotic birds and animals, including elephants.

1386 Cooper Road
Hamilton, ON
Canada N1R 5S2

CLEVELAND METROPARKS ZOO

African Elephant Crossing allows visitors to get up-close views of elephants.

33900 Wildlife Way
Cleveland, OH 44109

MARYLAND ZOO

Home to a family of African elephants, including Samson, who was born at the zoo in 2008.

1 Safari Place
Baltimore, MD 21217

WILDLIFE SAFARI

Visitors can drive through this 600-acre (243 ha) park filled with free-roaming animals.

1790 Safari Road
Winston, OR 97496

INDEX